POSTPARTUM DEPRESSION

DR. WILLIAM W. SLIDER

DR. JOHN WESLEY SLIDER, EDITOR

DEDICATION

To Mamie Ethel Osman Slider.

CONTENTS

ABSTRACT

An experiment was conducted to test the hypothesis that postpartum depression occurs most often among women following the birth of a female child. The secondary hypothesis was that this depression is a result of jealousy engendered by a sense of competition with a daughter.

One hundred mothers of recently born children were given a questionnaire of seventeen items. These items were focused on areas that could be factors in postpartum depression. While there was a strong indication of the incidence of depression among the mothers, there was not a preponderance of females born to those depressed nor was there any significant indication of jealousy as a factor in the depression.

1 CURRENT RESEARCH

One of the widely recognized areas of emotional illness and women is that associated with the time following childbirth. Many women suffer from acute attacks of emotional disturbance connected with childbirth. These reactions may occur at any time during pregnancy and throughout the first year following the birth of a child. The most common feature of postpartum emotional disturbance is generally depression. This depression may range from an exaggeration of usual feelings of worry to a severe condition. The mother may become exceedingly irritable and especially vulnerable to emotional frustrations. In some cases there is a psychotic condition related to the disturbance.[1]

The number of persons the affected is rather large, although the estimation of incidence covers a wide range. By about the third day postpartum, many women began to experience depression and periods of crying: "The baby blues," or postpartum depression. Often this lasts only a day or two, but it may continue for several weeks. Estimates of the number of women experiencing postpartum depression very from twenty-five to sixty-seven percent, depending on the study. Severe disturbance is rare. Postpartum psychosis occurs in about one in every 400 women.[2]

Other studies indicate that from twenty to forty percent of women report emotional disturbances or cognitive dysfunction in the early postpartum period.[3]

prior research in the general field of postpartum depression is recorded all the way back to the fourth century BC when Hippocrates studied the problem.

---

[1] Clyde M Narramore, *Encyclopedia of Psychological Problems* (1966), p193.

[2] Janet Sibley Hyde, Understanding Human Sexuality (1979), p115.

[3] Alfred Freedman, Harold Kaplan, and Benjamin Sadock, *Modern Synopsis of Psychiatry*, volume II (1980), p523.

He felt the cause of the sorrow or madness of the new mother was being caused by "… the bloody vaginal discharge that continues for some four weeks after a woman has given birth, being suppressed and diverged and transported to the woman's brain."[4]

This ancient physician was not entirely out of focus because with the birth of the baby the woman's body undergoes a drastic physiological change. During pregnancy the placenta produces high levels of both estrogen and progesterone. When the placenta is expelled, the levels of these hormones drop sharply; and thus the postpartum period is characterized by low levels of both estrogen and progesterone. The levels of these hormones gradually return to normal over a period of a few weeks to a few months. Other endocrine changes include an increase in hormones associated with breast-feeding.[5]

Since this early time most research in postpartum depression has been incidental in that it was in conjunction with some other study. The depression occurring to new mothers was regarded as "milk fever," "baby blues," or as just a peculiarity that could be summarized by this observation:

> *In the past, postpartum depression — irritability, anxiety, unrelieved sadness, tears, hostility to the baby, insatiable demands for the*

---

[4] Maggie Scarf, **Unfinished Business** (1980) p278.
[5] Hyde, op cit, p114.

husbands attention or antagonism toward him, and sexual retreat — have either been attributed to fear of the feminine role, cramps and cravings; or trivialized, as in an ad for hair coloring: "We had the postpartum blues. So we became blondes."[6]

Since there have been no studies related to the sex of the child in postpartum depression, a computer scan was run by Bibliographical Retrieval Services, Inc., in Scotia, New York, to discover past and present investigations of the subject. The results revealed a wide variety of recent articles that address some facet of this depression. There was, however, no research specifically directed to discovering the effect of the sex of the child in producing postpartum depression.

An hypothesis developed: The sex of the child must have a direct effect upon the emotional state of the mother because of the value placed upon the male child in various cultures. This value placed on the male child is revealed in previous research, such as Sigmund Freud's "penis envy" theory.

Of little girls we know they feel themselves handicapped by the absence of a large visible penis, and envy a boy's possession of it. From this source

---

[6] Letty C. Pogrebin, ***Growing Up Free*** (1980), p146.

primarily springs the wish to be a man that is resumed again later in the neurosis.[7]

The male value is also felt because of the present economic and social structures that give preference to the male sex in birth despite the feminism of the 1970s, the preference for a sign is stronger than ever.[8]

Another factor that may indicate a relationship to the sex of the child and postpartum depression is that couples whose first two children are girls are more likely to have a third child.[9] The birth of a female child may thus be depressing because of the implication that the mother must continue until a male is born.

A lower value for being female may thus have a bearing on the effect of the birth of a girl to a mother. Rejection of femininity along with sexual difficulties is also said to be associated with puerperal depression.[10]

---

[7] Sigmund Freud in Scarf, op cit., p278.

[8] N.E. Williamson, "Boys or Girls? Parents' Preferences and Sex Control," *Population Bulletin* (January 1978), p4.

[9] Citation unknown.

[10] R. Meares, J. Grimwards, and C. Wood, "A Possible Relationship between Anxiety in Pregnancy and Puerperal Depression," *Journal of Psychosomatic Research* (1976), pp605-610.

There is also a suggestion as to the effect of female births in producing the more serious emotional problems. For mothers who psychosis developed during gestation, researchers have found for males born in forty-one deliveries. When psychosis developed within one month of conception, only females were born.[11] It should be observed at this point that the reason for studies that show more female births in relation to psychosis is because the male fetus has a therapeutic or symptom-masking effect on schizophrenia.[12]

further incentive to research the effect of the sex of the child on postpartum depression came from a statement by Adrienne Rich expressing the desire she had felt to be male:

> *When I first became pregnant, I set my heart on a son. I wanted to give birth at twenty-five, to my unborn self, the self that our father-centered family had suppressed in me, someone independent, actively willing, original. If I wanted to give birth to myself as a male, it was because*

---

[11] C. Astrup, "Maternal Schizophrenia and the Sex of Offspring," **Biological Psychiatry** (October 1974), pp211-214.

[12] **Ibid.**

males seem to inherit those qualities by right of gender.[13]

It is reasonable to think that such a feeling in women would cause depression if a girl were to be born.

There is another facet that implies that boys may be preferred by the mother, and thus giving birth to a female may cause the mother depression. Females are sexually more vulnerable, require more supervision, and are more fragile. The implication is that more care is required on the part of the mother and there is more direct responsibility for a female child on the mother's part.

The general statistics add weight to the preference for boys. The first of such studies in 1933 indicated a preference for boy babies at the ratio of 165 to 100. The figures remain about the same today.[14] This research encourage the testing of the effect of the sex of the child in producing puerperal depression.

---

[13] Adrianne Rich, ***Of Woman Born: Motherhood as Experience and Institution*** (1976), p193.

[14] Williamson, op cit, p4.

WILLIAM W. SLIDER

2 A NEW LINE OF INVESTIGATION

There is one other factor to be considered. It is the hypothesis that the birth of a female child induced depression in the mother because of the feeling of competition for the father's attention. This hypothesis could further be defined as the mothers sense of jealousy at the presence of another female.

This new line of investigation presented itself as a valid field for testing. There is no instrument available for measuring the relationship of the sex of the child to postpartum depression; therefore, one was developed. There is one instance of "The Beck Depression Inventory"[15] being used in regard to

---

[15] The Beck Depression Inventory, created by Dr. Aaron T. Beck, is a twenty-one question, multiple-choice, self-report inventory. It is one of the most

postpartum emotional problems; but this instrument proved to be a general measurement for depression.

An instrument was prepared with an explanatory letter (appendices A and B). Seventeen questions were included that applied to areas where there were reported factors in postpartum depression. Some of the questions were used to mask the intention of the measurement.

Number nine on the questionnaire was prepared to gain a response to the effect of motherhood itself upon the subject and the question was based upon many observations summarized in this statement:

> *Women report the most psychiatric symptoms when they are immersed in their most roll-related activities: getting married, having babies, and caring for preschool children at home.*[16]

Research has indicated that mothers are often emotionally unprepared for their role. It is sometimes conceded that puerperal depression occurs in women who are ambivalent about their female roles and in particular the maternal role.[17]

---

widely used instruments for measuring the severity of depression.

[16] Pogrebin, op cit, p148.

[17] Meares, op cit, p610.

Question 11 was suggested by various articles. Whether a woman is reacting to her first baby or her fourth, she is not depressed by the baby; but by the concomitants of what are called "total motherhood" – the loss of freedom; lack of emotional support and economic autonomy; feelings of helplessness; the unassisted, incessant labor of childcare; fatigue; the sense of decreased sex appeal; low self-esteem; and the absence of a life of her own outside the home.[18]

Question 10 was inserted to waive the effect of the person's own mother upon their own emotional stability to be mothers. Although some women are committed to the mothering experience, their own childhood experiences lead them to reject their own mothers as models for imitation and identification. Their own mothers' maternal behavior increasingly becomes a reference or model for a new mother's own program of action.[19] Repudiation of the mothering role by the parent of a mother may often cause the new mother to reject her infant in turn.

Question seven was developed as a result of statements summarized in a report by a group of mothers in Toronto, Canada:

We found the loss of sleep was one of the major causes of depression. Most of us go through the first month in a stupor. We found that loss of

---

[18] Pogrebin, op cit, p146.
[19] Freedman, op cit, 524

sleep creates tension, and this in turn makes it harder to sleep. Many of us felt angry about this, but did not want to blame the baby, so we turned our anger to ourselves fearing that we were not good mothers and feeling guilty that we were not enjoying it more.[20]

The possibility of unwanted pregnancy as a factor in postpartum depression suggested question 12. There has been no study undertaken to determine the frequency of unwanted conceptions among patients with postpartum psychosis. One would expect that a positive correlation would be found in view of the tendency for most people to avoid situations they anticipate will be overwhelmingly stressful.[21]

Anticipation may also be an ingredient in puerperal depression. There may be produced anxiety and depression successively in the same individual. This observation might have some implications for research into the biological basis of non-psychotic mental illness.[22]

---

[20] C. Brown, "Baby Blues," **Nursing Mirror** (September 1975), pp61-2.

[21] Citation unknown.

[22] Meares, op cit, p610.

3 METHODOLOGY

The subjects of the study were one hundred females who had given birth within a two-year period. These subjects were selected from women's groups and from names listed in the birth column of local newspapers. The selection was preceded by the announcement of the time span allowed after the birth of the child (two years) and by presenting a letter that defined the purpose of the questionnaire – to determine factors in postpartum depression. A cover letter was sent with the questionnaire and the postage-paid return envelope was included.

No instrument had been developed for testing the incidence of postpartum depression as related to the sex of the child and the effect of the female child in creating jealousy on the part of the mother. A new instrument was designed. 17 questions were compiled and subjects were asked to complete them. Questions associated with the usual factors assumed to be involved in postpartum depression were included. In addition certain general questions were included to eliminate the possibility of predisposing the response of the subject to key questions. These questions were numbers five and 13. The results were arranged in tables and their significance determined by the "phi coefficient."[23]

---

[23] In statistics, the phi coefficient (also referred to as the "mean square contingency coefficient" and denoted by φ or r_φ) is a measure of association for two binary variables introduced by Karl Pearson.

4 RESULTS

The key questions in the analysis of results were one, five, and 13. Question one revealed the number of subjects who experienced depression. Sixty-one percent of the subjects experienced depression after giving birth and thirty-nine percent did not. The difference between the two sample proportions is significant at the .05 level. The absolute value of "Z" is also greater than 2.58 for the .01 level; so one may conclude that these two proportions are significantly different at both the five percent level and the one percent level.

Question five produced a number of those subjects depressed in relation to the sex of the child. A score of .12 was not high enough to indicate that the sex of the child had any bearing on the depression of the mother.

Question 13 revealed that only twelve of sixty-one subjects had any feelings of jealousy. Of these twelve, however, nine had female children and three had males. Using the test of significance between two sample proportions, the value of "Z" determined by the test was 2.449 which was significant at the five percent level, but was not significant at the one percent level.[24]

Table 1
Number of Mothers Experiencing Depression

Sex of the Child	Depressed Mothers	Not Depressed Mothers	Total
Female	25	21	46
Male	36	18	54
Total	61	39	100

---

[24] The null hypothesis in Question 13 is that the two proportions are the same ($\pi_1 = \pi_2$). In this case the observed difference between the two sample proportions is not significant and was attributed to chance or random sampling fluctuations. The alternative hypothesis is that the two sample proportions are different. In order to determine whether the two proportions are significantly different, the test of significance between the two sample proportions was performed.

5 DISCUSSION

The most significant finding in this study was the relatively high incidence of depression following childbirth (sixty-one percent). This high incidence indicates the importance of pursuing an investigation into the causes of postpartum depression with a view to finding the means to alleviate such emotional stress. Interestingly, there was no strong indication in this study that any of the classic causes felt to be a factor in postpartum depression were significant. The lack of sleep as a factor in this type of depression showed a .2854 [level,] which is not strong.

Table 2
Sleep Patterns of the Mothers

	Depressed	Not Depressed	Total
Broken Sleep	25	21	46
Normal Sleep	36	18	54
Total	61	39	100

The matter of the illness of the child as being important in effecting the mother toward depression was not significant at the .087 level. Whether or not the new mothers felt themselves prepared for their parenting was not significant with a .081 level.

Table 3
Emotionally Prepared to Be a Mother

	Depressed	Not Depressed	Total
Prepared	42	28	70
Not Prepared	19	11	30
Total	61	39	100

The image of "mothering" given by the new mother's own mother, and frequently mentioned by those studying the problem of postpartum depression, seemed of less significance than ordinarily indicated (.3217).

Table 4
Pattern for Mothering by Own Mother

	Depressed	Not Depressed	Total
Good	27	30	57
Poor	34	9	43
Total	61	39	100

The popular idea of "suburban housewife syndrome," or the "trapped mother," was discounted to a large degree by thirty-one of sixty-one of the subjects feeling that this was a factor in their depression.

Table 5
Felt Trapped by Motherhood

	Depressed	Not Depressed	Total
Felt Trapped	31	15	46
Did Not Feel Trapped	30	24	54
Total	61	39	100

The test for significance in relation to the number of those feeling jealousy and having female children was significant, but the number having a feeling of jealousy for all births was not significant.

Table 6
Did Birth of Child Cause Jealousy toward Husband?

	Depressed	Not Depressed	Total
Jealous	12	2	14
Not Jealous	49	37	86
Total	61	39	100

The relationship of anticipating depression and realizing the depression was at the same figure as the "trapped" feeling.

Table 7
Were Emotional Problems Anticipated?

	Depressed	Not Depressed	Total
Anticipated	31	5	36
Not Anticipated	30	24	54
Total	61	39	100

The lack of strong statistical support for any of the psychologically related causes for postpartum depression suggests the possibility of the causes being related to biological factors – or more properly, to emotional stresses engendered by biological influences.

Obviously the predictions of a strong significance of the birth of a female child and the jealousy of the mother toward a female child in postpartum depression were not supported. This lack of support could be attributed to an inadequate instrument or flawed testing.

WILLIAM W. SLIDER

REFERENCES

Astrup, C., "Maternal Schizophrenia and the Sex of Offspring," **Biological Psychiatry** (October 1974), pp211 – 214.

Brown, C., "Baby Blues," **Nursing Mirror** (September 1975), pp61 – 62.

Freedman, Alfred; Kaplan, Harold; Sadock, Benjamin; **Modern Synopsis of Psychiatry**, volume II (1980).

Hyde, Janet Shibley, **Understanding Human Sexuality** (1979).

Lowenstein, H., "Post-Puerperal Depression," *American Journal of Psychiatry* (November 1968), p707.

Meares, R.; Grimwade, J.; Wood, C.; "A Possible Relationship between Anxiety in Pregnancy and Puerperal Depression," *Journal of Psychosomatic Research* (1976), pp605 – 610.

Narramore, Clyde M., *Encyclopedia of Psychological Problems* (1966).

Pogrebin, Letty C., *Growing Up Free* (1980).

Scarf, Maggie, *Unfinished Business: Pressure Points in the Lives of Women* (1980).

Williamson, N.E., "Boys or Girls? "Parents Preferences and Sex Control," *Population Bulletin* (January 1978), p4.

APPENDIX A
QUESTIONAIRE COVER LETTER

Christ Church, United Methodist

4614 BROWNSBORO ROAD
LOUISVILLE, KY. 40207

WILLIAM W. SLIDER
MINISTER

PHONE
897-6421
897-6422

February, 1981

Mothers often report depression following childbirth (postpartum depression). This can vary from having no problem, to very mild instances, to those severe enough to need hospitalization. The occurence of this depression is reported in enough instances to merit investigation as to contributing factors.

We have prepared a questionnaire with the purpose of discovering some of those factors which seem to be present in most postpartum depression. This has been initiated with the thought that a more thorough knowledge of the subject will be helpful in addressing the problem. The project is in conjunction with research for the graduate Degree in Psychology.

The questionnaire will take only a few minutes to complete. There is no way to identify the respondent. Do not sign your name and thus complete anonymity is guaranteed. A postage paid addressed envelope is enclosed for your convenience.

Thank you very much for your assistance.

Sincerely,

William W. Slider

William W. Slider, Th.D., D.D.

WWS/lt

APPENDIX B
QUESTIONAIRE

WILLIAM W. SLIDER

<u>QUESTIONNAIRE CONCERNING FACTORS IN POSTPARTUM DEPRESSION</u>

1. Did you experience depression after the birth of your child?

    YES_____   NO_____

2. What was the birth order?

    (First child, second, etc.) _____

3. Was the depression: Mild_____ Moderate_____ Severe_____

4. Did treatment require professional care?

    (Such as psychiatrist, psychologist, hospitalization)

    _____

5. What was the sex of the child?

    Male_____   Female_____

6. Was the father supportive of you during the period following the birth?

    Yes_____   No_____

7. Was your sleep pattern disturbed during this time?

    Little_____   Some_____   Greatly_____

8. Was the child ill during this period?

    Normal_____   Seriously_____

9. Do you feel you were emotionally prepared to be a mother?

    Yes_____   No_____

10. Do you feel your own mother gave you a good pattern for "mothering"? (Was
    your experience with her one which would be positive when you became a mother?)
    Completely_____   Somewhat_____   Poor_____

11. Was there a sense of being "trapped" in that you felt you were confined to caring for this infant for an extended time?

Yes_____ No_____

12. Was the child "planned" in that you had made a decision to have a child?

Yes_____ No_____

13. Did the birth of the child cause you some feeling of jealousy in that he/she would infringe on your relationship to your husband?

Yes_____ No_____

14. If you have more than the one child, did you feel somewhat the same depression after each birth?

Yes_____ No_____ In some cases_____

15. How many children do you have? _____

Male_____ Female_____

16. Did you anticipate any sort of emotional upset after the birth of your child?

Yes_____ No_____ Perhaps_____

17. Were you or your husband disappointed in the sex of your child?

You_____ Husband_____

WILLIAM W. SLIDER

ABOUT THE AUTHOR AND EDITOR

This brief work on postpartum depression was submitted by Dr. William W. Slider as a part of his Master of Science studies in Psychology at Spalding College – now Spalding University. The paper was presented on April 29, 1981. Dr. Slider was sixty-three years old.

Dr. William W. Slider, A.A., B.A., M.A., M.S., S.T.M., D.D., Th.D., was a United Methodist pastor in Louisville, Kentucky. Dr. Slider, who passed away in 2001, was married to Jean Elizabeth Wells Slider, who followed him to heaven in 2008.

Dr. Slider served as pastor of Christ Church, United Methodist, for twenty-five years. From the pulpit of Christ Church he had a significant impact on generations of members, the community, and his family.

Bill and Jean Slider had two sons. The elder son, John is married to Lillian. They have two children, Heather and William.

The younger son, Robert, is married to Laura. They have two children, Diana and Ian.

Dr. Slider has other works that are published posthumously. They may be found at VirtualChurchResources.org.

The editor of this brief book and other books by Dr. William Slider is John Slider. Dr. John Wesley Slider, B.A., M.Div., D.Min., was a United Methodist pastor from 1979 until his retirement in 2010, when he transferred his ordination to the Free Methodist Church. He is currently the pastor of Breckenridge Chapel, Free Methodist, in Saint Matthews (Louisville), Kentucky.

John is married to Lillian Natalia Stewart Slider. Their daughter, Heather, is married to Michael, and they have a son, Matthew. John and Lillian's son, William, is married to Tina.

In addition to editing his father's books, John has several books of his own published.

www.ingramcontent.com/pod-product-compliance
Lightning Source LLC
Chambersburg PA
CBHW071327310526
45789CB00016B/1687